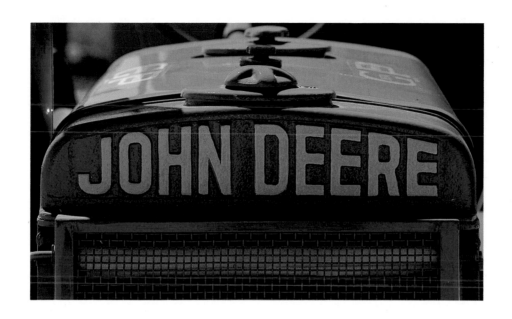

The John Deere Tractor

Randy Leffingwell

MBI Publishing Company

This edition published in 2002 by MBI Publishing Company, Galtier Plaza, Suite 200, 380 Jackson Street, St. Paul, MN 55101-3885 USA

MBI Publishing Company books are also available at discounts in bulk quantity for industrial or sales-promotional use. For details write to Special Sales Manager at Motorbooks International Wholesalers & Distributors, Galtier Plaza, Suite 200, 380 Jackson Street, St. Paul, MN 55101-3885 USA.

Library of Congress Cataloging-in-Publication Data Available

ISBN 0-7603-1377-6

Printed in China

Contents

Chapter 1

From Plows to Tractors

All-Wheel Drive to the Waterloo Boy

By the time Deere & Company entered the farm tractor market it was the last of the major agricultural equipment and implement manufacturers to join the business. Whereas Deere & Company felt comfortable innovating seed drills, hay rakes, and of course, improving founder John Deere's steel plows, it was considerably less sure of itself with regard to tractors. This caution mirrored a hereditary Deere family trait and continued a characteristic evolved from the founder himself. Following several years of soul-searching and hand-wringing by the board of directors, a series of development prototypes were authorized. These designs, which were extensively tested and met with lesser or greater success, mimicked or copied the competition of the day.

John Deere was born in Rutland, Vermont, on February 7, 1804. Uninterested in continuing formal education, he left college to apprentice with a local blacksmith. The practical education Deere received there—learning the high value of quality workmanship—stayed with him throughout his life. His apprenticeship ended in 1825, he married two years later, and after several frustrating years of producing good work but struggling to make ends meet, he and his family moved west in late 1836 to Grand Detour, Illinois, a growing community on the Rock River 100 miles west of Chicago.

The soil around Grand Detour plagued local farmers who had also emigrated from the East Coast. Back in New England cast iron plows scoured clean, that is, the soil spilled off cleanly, but the gumbo around the Rock River clung

1918 All-Wheel Drive

First tested in spring 1916, Deere's All-Wheel Drive tractor pulled 3,000 pounds in field tests. This example, believed to be the oldest complete restored John Deere tractor, number 191879, is owned by Frank Hansen of Rollingstone, Minnesota. It used a 4.50x5.00in bore and stroke four-cylinder upright engine designed for Deere & Company by Walter McVicker. It rated 12/24 horsepower, and only 100 were manufactured.

1915 Waterloo Boy Model R

Waterloo Gasoline Engine Company produced the Waterloo Boy from 1912 through 1924. This Model R, built in 1915, used the horizontally mounted two-cylinder 5.50x7.00in bore and stroke engine that set the style for all John Deere tractor engines until 1960. Ken Kass of Dunkerton, Iowa, owns this example, number 1643. Something like 25,722 Waterloo Boy tractors were built.

tightly to the plows. Farmers were forced to stop and scrape the plows frequently during spring planting. These farmers had already used Deere's blacksmith skills, and they vented their frustration to him.

Deere knew metal and understood its characteristics. Visiting a sawmill owner one day, he spotted a broken steel saw blade that had been polished bright by thousands of board feet of lumber cuts. Deere asked for the blade, returned to his shop, cut off the teeth, and formed it to a plow moldboard. When a local farmer tested it and it plowed cleanly through the sticky soil, Deere's new career was launched. It was 1838.

Within another five years, he had a partner, had relocated to Moline, Illinois, had opened a factory, and had produced and sent out the door the first ten production plows. His son Charles joined the firm in 1853, having finished school in accounting and business practices. Charles' skills with money matched his enthusiasm for his father's products. In 1857, even as he was out in the fields assisting in new product demonstrations and learning from the farmers what else the company could do for them, he was named its vice president.

Beginning in 1869 the company was opening branch offices throughout the Midwest. Deere & Company had added cultivators, harrows, seed drills, wagons, and buggies to its line of steel plows. Deere even followed the bicycle craze in the 1890s, marketing another maker's two-wheeler under its own name. Implement catalogs showed not only single- and two-bottom plows but also four- and six-gang plows as

well. It showed steam traction engines dragging its big plows across unbroken sod.

The new century brought new challenges. John Deere had died in 1886 and Charles had become president. His biggest threat came from the newly merged conglomeration in Chicago known as International Harvester Corporation, formed in 1902. IHC began circling around Deere & Company. It tried to acquire smaller companies and made offers on some with which Deere had agreements. Reacting quickly, Deere acquired some of its own suppliers, among them Dain Manufacturing. Dain, in Ottumwa, Iowa, produced hay harvesting equipment and its acquisition brought onto Deere's board a new vice president, a forward-looking innovator, Joseph Dain, Sr.

Five years of the stress of battling with International Harvester eventually cost Charles Deere his life. He had run Deere & Company for nearly fifty years and had taken the company from being a reputable plow manufacturer to being one of the two major agricultural implement makers and distributors in the United States.

Charles Deere was succeeded by his son-in-law, William Butterworth, a lawyer. Butterworth was an able heir; his instincts paralleled his late father-in-law and so did his challenges. Deere & Company still had holes in its product lineup; most noticeably it had no harvesters. Following several serious efforts—including a bid to acquire J. I. Case—and fielding off an attempt from IHC to acquire Deere & Company, Butterworth began to buy up a number of smaller manufacturers.

And just when Butterworth and the board of directors thought they could catch their breath, farmers got caught up by the automobile. Deere and the other implement makers quickly saw that while they had to accept time payments from farmers to buy their products, the same farmers went out and paid cash for automobiles. Mechanization was coming to the farm and it was driving itself.

International Harvester responded quickly. It introduced its first tractor in 1906. J. I. Case had produced steam traction engines since the 1890s and was working with a Case relative to produce the Wallis tractor by 1910. However, by this time, IHC "owned" the tractor business. Deere board members were scattered like hand-sown seed on the issue of building a Deere tractor.

As early as 1910, Deere stated in its catalogs that the Gas Traction Company's Big Four Model 30 was "its" tractor. Deere tried to acquire the company but was outbid. Other makers' tractors filled in Deere's catalogs but the question became clear: When would Deere & Company produce its own?

In early 1912 a divided board of directors finally charged the company's engineer C. H. Melvin with the task of producing a prototype tractor. Board members dictated that it must not only pull plows but that it also must be capable of other agricultural functions. President and chairman William Butterworth was loudest in his cautions. The development costs worried him; he had seen other well-known, previously solid companies fail after costly attempts didn't produce successful tractors.

Melvin's prototype justified all of Butterworth's fears. It was neither strong enough nor reliable. After two years of repeated testing and modification, it was scrapped. But Joe Dain refused to let the idea die. He began working on a new design, and within six months he presented his case well enough that the board funded his project. His target was a tractor that Deere could sell for $700. Six months later, in March 1916, his all-wheel-drive tricycle received board approval to begin regular production as Deere & Company's first tractor.

Dain's machine was a reversed tricycle; its two front wheels steered. All three wheels were powered by a collection of chains, driveshafts, and universal joints. Dain's first engine selection didn't produce enough power, so Walter McVicker, an independent engineer, was conscripted to design a new four-cylinder engine for the Deere tractor. Tests in the field showed that the 4,000 pound tractor could pull 3,000 pounds through average soil conditions. Production costs were higher than first anticipated, however, and the price was set at $1,200. Production was authorized for the first 100 units to be built in the Marseilles Works (Deere's binder factory) in East Moline, Illinois. The board then considered plans for a second production run and quickly recognized other considerations. Additional manufacturing facilities were urgently needed.

In Waterloo, Iowa, about 110 miles west of Moline, the board found a plant with a foundry, warehouse, and manufacturing space and additional undeveloped land. And they found an existing tractor. The Waterloo Gasoline Engine

Company had begun producing tractors in 1913 but had first experimented with them in 1892. At that time, a traveling thresherman named John Froelich had completed his first experimental self-propelled tractor. In the next four years, Froelich produced four more of his machines but sold only two. Problems plagued them and both were returned to him, determined to be failures by their buyers.

Froelich's partners would no longer support his single-minded obsession with self-propulsion whereas they knew his engines worked and could be sold profitably for stationary uses. Froelich left, and the partners formed Waterloo Gasoline Engine Company, manufacturing horizontal two-cylinder engines.

The pressures of the marketplace led them back to tractor experiments when two new engineers joined the firm: Louis Witry as engine designer, and Harry Leavitt, who began experimenting with crawler applications. In 1913 the firm introduced its Waterloo Boy One Man Tractor. Witry and Leavitt continued developing new and improved models. A single-forward speed Model R was introduced in 1914, supplemented with a two-speed Model N in 1917. Both used the same two-cylinder 12-horsepower engine (producing 25 horsepower on the belt pulley), and it was this fully developed Model N that Deere & Company executives examined on their visits to the Waterloo plant in early 1918.

Deere's directors reviewed the possibilities and authorized the Waterloo purchase on

1920 Waterloo Boy Model T
Waterloo produced portable engines from 1920 through mid-1925. This example, number 1056, used the 6.50x7.00in bore and stroke Model N tractor engine. Horsepower was only rated for the belt pulley—25 horsepower—since this engine was not self-propelled. It is owned by Lester Layher of Wood River, Nebraska. Fewer than 390 of these portable engines were manufactured.

March 14, 1918, for $2.35 million. With the purchase, Deere acquired not only a functioning tractor production factory but also the outstanding orders for new tractors. In addition, they inherited the research and development that Witry and Leavitt had done on a replacement for their Waterloo Boy.

Deere suddenly had no reason to continue production after the first 100 of its own Joe Dain-designed Deere All-Wheel Drive tractors.

Chapter 2

The Tractor is Here to Stay

The Model D

Waterloo had also begun work on a successor to its Waterloo Boy Model N. Each prototype effort was lettered alphabetically when improvements generated a new model. When Witry got to the fourth incarnation he stopped. Waterloo was satisfied with its new model. And so was its new owner, Deere & Company. But World War I—and Henry Ford—interrupted plans for the company to quickly introduce its Model D.

Henry Ford's Fordson tractor arrived in the marketplace after more than a decade of testing at Ford's Dearborn, Michigan, farm. The lightweight (2,710 pounds), affordable ($785), compact machine quickly stole the sales lead from International Harvester; Ford eventually decimated Waterloo Boy and Deere & Company. It was not that Ford's tractor was so good, it was simply so affordable and so available. Ford's auto dealerships sold Fordson tractors on the same floor as the cars, and during the ultimately ruinous price war against International Harvester, Henry Ford

reduced his tractor price to $395 in 1921. Deere could go no lower than $890.

Inadvertently, however, Ford contributed to Deere's one success during that period, an effect that lasted much longer than Ford's price reduction. By 1920, more than 180 companies were claiming to manufacture farm tractors in the United States. Of those, many produced poor quality machines designed more to take the farmer's money than to pull the plow. One such machine was sold to a Nebraska legislator who was in a position to do something about it.

A firm in Minneapolis hired an engineer named Ford and thereby felt entitled to call its

1923 Model D
The Model D engine was about the only thing Waterloo Gasoline Engine Co. retained in its redesign. This used the Model N 6.50x7.00in bore and stroke horizontal two-cylinder engine, producing 12/25 horsepower and driving through the same two-speed transmission. Only fifty were produced in exactly this configuration.

1923 Model D
This 1923 Model D, number 30410, is one of the earliest-known two-cylinder Deere tractors: it was the tenth built. With its 26in spoked flywheel, its ladder-side radiator, and its fabricated front axle, it replaced the Waterloo Boy tractors. It is owned by Lester Layer of Wood River, Nebraska.

1927 Model D

By late 1927, Deere had made numerous changes and improvements to the Model D. Engine bore had increased from 6.50in to 6.75in, though power output remained the same. A solid splined flywheel was used. "Road rims" were an option available for farmers who needed to transport their tractors over pavement.

tractor a "Ford." Its copyrights and patents blocked Henry Ford from using his own name—hence Fordson tractors, named after Henry Ford & Son. The Nebraska lawmaker, Wilmot Crozier, bought the wrong Ford, which broke immediately. He replaced it with a Rumely, which never broke. This caused Crozier to wonder how many more makers offered value for money and if there was some way either to enforce reliability or at least to test for it. The Nebraska Tractor Tests were begun as a result, consisting of a set of strictly monitored trials. The law stated that any maker wishing to offer a tractor for sale in Nebraska had to submit to these tests and the results would be made public record.

Deere's Waterloo Boy Model N was the first tractor submitted and tested. It passed with flying colors in April 1920. Still, the Waterloo Boy looked like an old-style tractor compared to Ford's Fordson. Louis Witry and Harry Leavitt had the new tractor in development and testing at the time. It was another few years—not until 1923 to be exact—before the last prototype was produced and manufacture of the first 1,000 Model D tractors was authorized. It was a long distance from the board's first agonized step with 100 All-Wheel Drive tractors. But it accurately reflected the marketplace and Deere & Company's confidence in its new machine.

The Model D was smaller, lighter, and more maneuverable than the Waterloo Boy had been. Well-regarded by farmers, it met with success; sales and production of the $1,000 Model D increased slowly but steadily.

The first Model Ds differed from the Waterloo Boy in several obvious ways. Steering was moved to the operator's left side, and the wheel was directly linked to the front axle. A 26in diameter spoked flywheel replaced Waterloo's solid one. But the flywheel and many other pieces were in constant evolution. The 880th Model D featured a smaller (24in), heavier, spoked flywheel, and two years later it was replaced again with a solid one. The first fifty Model Ds used the "ladder" front axle, which appeared to have been fabricated and pieced together from an assortment of steel rods and plates left over from other projects. It was not strong; beginning with the fifty-first copy, tractors used cast front axles, which offered greater strength as well as additional weight on the front end.

The two-cylinder engine carried over from the Model N Waterloo Boys into the first several years of Model D. It was enlarged in 1927 from 6.5 to 6.75in cylinder bore. Deere began exporting its tractors that year, primarily to Russia and Argentina. In 1931, Deere moved the steering back to the right side, connected by a worm and gear system.

1927 Model D
Frank Bettancourt of Vernalis, California, owns this late 1927 example, number 54132. The Model D remained in production from 1923 through 1953, and slightly more than 113,000 were manufactured in this Unstyled version through 1938. At introduction in 1924, the tractors sold for $1,000.

Chapter 3

Developing the First Row Crop Tractors

Models C, GP, A and B

While farm tractors had shrunk to something an individual could operate without assistance, the machines were still limited in their uses. Most tractors were effective only for soil breaking, first planting, and crop harvesting. The interim—and important—cultivating between crop rows was not yet possible. The design of the tractors simply made maneuvering through tall, narrow crop rows impossible without doing nearly as much damage as good. Operator visibility—to see the sharp cultivator knives cutting weeds but not crops—was not adequate. The view downward was obstructed by the tractor itself.

International Harvester responded first. Its Farmall had higher ground clearance and greater rear tread width than its competitors' tractors. Its front wheels, placed nearly beside each other and canted on opposing angles, slipped through the rows while reinforcing the ground shape. IHC placed its cultivator in front of the tractor, the better to see its direc-

tion and progress. The tractor was introduced for $825.

Deere had begun work on its own row crop tractor, known internally as the Model C. To speed up development, Deere retained the standard front end of its Model D. Theo Brown, head of the experimental department, then conceived a three-row cultivator where the tractor straddled the center row.

It was a controversial idea. IHC's Farmall with its tricycle configuration cultivated four rows. Its wide rear axle encompassed two rows. Deere board members felt sales would be lost to the competition if its machine did only three-

1928 Model C

The Model C was Deere's first attempt at a general purpose row-crop tractor. Only 112 prototypes were assembled before the problems they revealed led to yet another model, the GP-WT. This example, number 200109, is likely to be the oldest John Deere row-crop tractor known to exist. It belongs to Walter and Bruce Keller of Kaukauna, Wisconsin.

1929 Model GP
The GPs were introduced in 1928, following tests and development of the Model C experimentals. This 1929 example, number 208761, used Deere's 5.75x6.00in bore and stroke engine, which was replaced in 1930 by the 6.00x6.00 two-cylinder. Frank Bettancourt owns this GP, fitted with rubber tires on cut-down steel wheels. Between 1928 and 1930, nearly 23,600 GPs were manufactured with the 5.75x6.00in engine, rating 10 drawbar and 20 belt pulley horsepower.

fourths as much work. The company agonized; the Farmall was in production, thousands had sold. Deere's dealers were crying for a row crop tractor. A complete redesign would take two years. The loss of business would be irrevocable. The board reasoned that the Model C could evolve as the Model D had done during its production run.

One last concern that affected Deere was caused by an industry completely unrelated to agriculture. Telephone lines with pin-drop clarity were a dream of the future in 1928. Dealers and factory personnel worried that an order for Model C tractors could be misunderstood as an order for Model Ds. So Deere decided to call its new tractor the GP (General Purpose) to avoid confusion over the phone.

By October 1928, GP production was twenty-five per day. It was selling but management heard that it was underpowered compared to

20

1929 Model GP

The GP followed the basic design of the Model D, but it was intended for row-crop uses and so the high-arched front axle was fitted. Deere's GPs were designed to operate as three-row tractors for planting, cultivating, and seeding. This was an unpopular configuration, and it was supplemented with a tricycle two- or four-row tractor in 1929. The GP was introduced for an $800 purchase price and offered a three-speed transmission. On steel wheels, it weighed 3,600 pounds.

the Farmall and that its three-row cultivator was a failure. Theo Brown was put back to work, and after a frantic year, Deere's Farmall clone appeared: the GP-WT, General Purpose-Wide Tread. Twenty-three prototypes tested successfully in early 1929, and the tractor was immediately offered for sale.

Henry Ford had quit the tractor business a year before. The price war he waged put dozens of others out too, leaving only the strongest and most innovative to survive. Ford's Fordson had failings that became more apparent as the others improved. This killed Ford's mass-production machine. Both Deere and International Harvester learned from the battle with Ford. Each streamlined its production and improved its product. At midyear 1929, IHC was the number one producer and Deere was number two.

Deere's GP tractors continued to evolve and improve, as the board expected. When Brown completed the GP-WT, he was given a new task, to produce a Model A and B, two new machines to supplement the D and GP.

Tractor power is described by the number of plows the machine can pull. For example, the Model D was a three-plow rated tractor, while the GP was rated for two plows. Actual engine output was quoted in two figures: horsepower

1935 Model B
Deere announced the Model B in late 1934 as a two-plow companion to the three-plow Model A introduced in 1933. Delivered on steel, the Model B weighed 3,275 pounds while the Model A weighed slightly more than 4,000 pounds. This tractor, number 11328, is owned by Herc Bouris of Sun City, California.

23

developed at the implement drawbar was quoted first, followed by output measured off the belt pulley. Waterloo Boy Model Ns and Deere Model Ds rated 12/25 horsepower; the new two-plow Model A produced 16/23 horsepower when it was introduced in 1934; the Model B, called a one-plow tractor, was rated at 9/14 horsepower when it arrived in 1935.

Both new tractors featured adjustable rear tread width to accommodate the variety of crops raised anywhere in the United States. Hydraulic power replaced mechanical implement lift. The two-cylinder engine was reengineered to burn virtually any fuel: it started on gasoline, and when operating temperature was reached the tank could be switched to kerosene or any other inexpensive fuel available. In 1937, high-clearance models were introduced, meant for cultivating or harvesting tomatoes, cotton, corn, or sugar cane. The tractors were lowered for other crops and to protect low-hanging fruit in orchards. All the moving parts were enclosed in striking sheet metal resembling streamlined racing cars.

Soil conditions affected tractor design as much as crop variety. Farmer/operators became important elements in the continuing development of agricultural equipment. Their experi-

1935 Model BN
Introduced in 1935, the Model BN specified a single front tire. Deere originally marketed this tractor as just the right size for the farmer's vegetable garden. Originally sold on steel, many farmers quickly converted them to rubber by cutting down steel wheels and welding on new rims.

ences, reported to the dealers, were passed back to the manufacturers; sometimes factory engineers went to see firsthand. In some instances the factory eventually adopted the ideas; in rarer instances they hired the innovators and even bought their companies.

In the Pacific Northwest, Jesse Lindeman and his brothers adapted crawler tracks first to Model D and then to GP tractors, which they sold to orchard owners for use in the sandy soil around Yakima, Washington. Lindeman's reputation was made when Deere introduced the Model B Orchard variant, the BO. Lindeman produced only six D and twenty-four GP crawlers through 1935. But by the time the BO went out of production, Lindeman had produced 1,675 little crawlers.

1935 Model B
Tests on the Model B were completed at Nebraska in April 1935. The horizontal twin-cylinder engine displaced 4.25x5.25in bore and stroke. At 1150rpm, it produced 11.8 drawbar horsepower and 15.1 on the pulley. Rear tread width was adjustable from 48in to 84in. Regular, industrial, and orchard versions were offered.

1935 Model BN

The Model Bs used Deere's 4.25x5.25in bore and stroke engine and the earliest Bs used a short frame. Deere specified a Wico Model X magneto and a Schebler DLTX70 carburetor. Power output was rated at 11.8 drawbar and 16 pulley horsepower. This example, number 1793, is owned by Frank Bettancourt

Left
1935 Model BN

"B Garden" tractors were not intended for the bean fields but with a Model B614 front tool carrier bar, they would have performed well.

*N*ow you can do all your farming work with mechanical power.... All operations are accomplished quickly, economically and efficiently with the John Deere General-Purpose Farm Tractor

—Model GP brochure

1935 Model BN
This is one of twelve BNs originally shipped to the San Francisco sales branch, which vigorously promoted their use for strawberries and other central California crops.

1935 Model BN

At that time, all John Deere tractors ran on kerosene, sometimes known as "stove top." It cost the farmer about six cents per gallon and made operating a John Deere tractor very economical. The Model B used the same four-speed transmission offered with the Model A, yielding a top speed of 6.25mph.

Left
1935 Model BN

John Boehm's 1935 BN, number 1799, rests near the family garden in Woodland, California, closer to its intended uses. This is another of the twelve first shipped to San Francisco in 1935. BN tractors were offered from 1935 through 1940, although exact production figures are not precise.

T here is nothing complicated or mystifying about this tractor or equipment. It is simple, understandable, and practical
—Model GP-WT brochure

1935 Model BN

John Boehm's 1935 BN, number 1799. Early Model B tractors used a prototype housing to attach the front axle to the frame, holding it with only four large bolts. Soon after introduction, Deere improved the mount, using eight bolts.

1935 Model GP-O

Jesse Lindeman in Yakima, Washington, began converting Deere tractors to crawlers to work better in central Washington's sandy soil. In 1935, he produced twenty-four of these GP crawlers, modifying the front and rear axles from production GP-Orchard models. This example, number 15704, belongs to Lester Layher.

1936 Model BW-40
The 40in row width was meant for sugar beets or tomato beds. All the Model BW-40 tractors were sold with square-edged rear fenders. But nearly all were removed by the operators because the fenders made getting onto the tractor nearly impossible by narrowing the leg room.

Right
1936 Model BW-40
Introduced in 1935 at the same time as the BN, this Model BW—B-Wide—only designated a "wide" front axle. Wide, in this case, was 40in. John Boehm's spindly looking 1936 BW, number 27097, was the seventh of seven preproduction prototypes with the 40in-narrow front and rear axles.

1936 Model BW-40

Mounting the front axle shaft to the frame with eight bolts was much stronger than the previous versions using only four. The Model B tractors were rated at two 14in plows and were fitted with a four-speed transmission capable of 6.25mph.

Right

1937 Model BI

The Model B was offered as an Industrial, although between 1936 and 1941 only 181 were produced. This version, number 326766, belongs to Don Merrihew of Mt. Pleasant, Michigan. Fitted with a Parsons Plow, manufactured in Newton, Iowa, this tractor was first shipped to Syracuse, New York, in the winter of 1936.

1937 Model AOS
In 1935, Deere introduced the A-Orchard and from 1936 through 1940 offered the "streamline" variation. This example, number 1319, began life as an engine experiment model, number 103, and has an oil dipstick located behind the flywheel. This tractor is owned by Walter and Bruce Keller.

1938 Model ANH

The ANH was the stronger, taller big brother to the Model BN. This example, number 472957, owned by Walter and Bruce Keller, was a late production model, with an enclosed radiator fan shaft. Model A tractors brought on-board hydraulics—the pump powered by the gearbox—to Deere customers.

Left

1938 Model ANH

The Model A-Hi-Crop tractors, in narrow or wide fronts, were produced only in 1937 and 1938. The Model A was a three-row tractor, using Deere's 5.50x6.50in bore and stroke engine. Horsepower output was 18.7 at the drawbar and 24.7 on the belt pulley.

1938 Model BWH
Walter and Bruce Keller's widest B-Hi-Crop stretches across 86.75in of front and rear track width. Their 1938 BWH, number 57718, is fitted with front axle extensions to encompass double crop rows.

Right
1938 Model BWH-40
John Boehm's 1938 Model BWH-40 stands tall in the late afternoon California sun. This tractor, number 55695, was one of probably only a dozen BWH-40s manufactured, and one of only fifty-one BWHs produced. Weaver Tractor Company of Sacramento pushed the BWH-40s, aggressively promoting them to farmers in central California.

Previous pages
1938 Model BWH-40
Operating the BWH-40 was hairy. It pitched and yawed dramatically over deeply furrowed fields. In addition, the frame was lengthened 5in over the 1935 through 1937 models. While that lessened the forward pitching, it seemed to exaggerate the sideways motion.

1938 Model BWH-40
Pneumatic rubber tractor tires were introduced in 1931 for between $50 and $200 per set and were optional with most manufacturers within a year or so. By the late 1930s, most farmers were accustomed to the improved ride and traction, which proved to be a problem during World War II when rubber was unavailable.

1939 Model AOS

John Boehm's 1939 Model AOS, number 1731, was one of approximately 815 produced. While Henry Dreyfuss had begun work with Deere & Co. in August 1937, the "streamline" A-Orchards were not the work of his designers. Orchard tractors sheet metal was meant to protect the crops from the tractor rather than the tractor from the crops.

1939 Model AOS
Separate rear wheel brakes provided for maneuverability in the trees. The tractors were 120in long and 55in wide and tall. Model AOS tractors used many parts that differed from the AO, also available through the same period, so AOS tractors used different serial numbers out of the regular Model A sequence.

1939 Model AOS
The early AO tractor did not incorporate a radiator grille guard, which appeared with the introduction of the AOS in 1936. The air intake and exhaust were removed from the hood and vented through the side. Exhaust in some versions was piped beneath the tractor and out the rear.

Far left
1939 Model AOS
Orchard tractors lowered the operator's seating position by several inches to allow clearance below the branches of fruit and nut trees. In addition, a fairing was installed to swing branches clear of the rear tires. Another kept branches from catching on spark plug wires.

Chapter 4

Styling Comes to the Tractor
Styled Models A and B

While the Lindeman brothers were changing Deere tractors mechanically, another outsider changed Deere tractors every other way. Three thousand miles across the United States, industrial designer Henry Dreyfuss was contacted by Deere engineers for help in making their tractors "more saleable." The engineers knew they had a good product, but branch dealers reported that farmers' wives were helping to make critical decisions on high-cost purchases. A finished appearance, a product with an air of quality workmanship, a design with an element of style was what pushed the sale from one product to another. Deere engineers understood that if two items perform identically but one looks better, buyers will be attracted to the better looking one.

Henry Dreyfuss had redesigned the telephone, an object every implement dealer knew well. Dreyfuss believed that a well-designed product performed better and offered less risk to operate, cost less to produce, instilled a sense of

value—and desire—in its purchaser, and looked better than its predecessor. He took to the John Deere product line quickly and enthusiastically. The results redefined farm tractors as much as Henry Ford had done twenty years earlier. Ford introduced the term "mass produced" to farm tractor manufacture, and Dreyfuss' work brought the word "styled" to farm tractor jargon.

In August 1937, Dreyfuss produced designs for the visual and mechanical improvement of Deere's Model A and B tractors. His designers narrowed the gas tank and radiator cowling to improve visibility forward and downward. The instrument panel was reorganized to make it

1939 Model BWH Styled
Deere went to the 4.50x5.50in bore and stroke engine during the first two years of Styled B production—an increase from the 4.25x5.25in engine offered previously. The four-speed transmission was also carried over, offering a top speed of 6.75mph for transport.

1939 Model BWH Styled
In 1938, Deere introduced the Styled Model B tractors in many but not all configurations. Between introduction of the Unstyled B in 1935 and 1952 when the Styled versions were finally taken out of production, nearly 310,000 were produced. Of those, fewer than fifteen—perhaps only six or eight—Styled BWHs were produced.

more readable and logical to the operator bouncing through the fields. The power takeoff and hydraulic fittings at the rear end were reorganized and tidied up, which made it easier for a hurried operator to recognize functions and fittings. The seat was redesigned to provide better posture and to make it easier for the operator to stand when visibility required it. When the Styled A and B tractors were introduced for 1938, the dealers were excited; they finally had something dramatically "new and improved" to sell. The farmers were somewhat less vocal in their enthusiasm.

Because its customers were a cautious group, Deere & Company continued to produce its Unstyled tractors, and it continued to introduce new variations only for Unstyled versions. Industrial tractors first appeared at the factory in

1926 when a Model D was fitted with solid rubber tires to perform shop work. A few of these DI tractors were offered for sale as well.

Industrial tractor operators usually spent more time seated than standing. The lowered seating position as well as the regular front axle—and even the exhaust and air intake configurations—were adopted from orchard tractors. In 1937, Deere & Company offered DI, AI, and BI tractors. Drilled plates welded to the frames were meant to hold scoop shovels, rotary sweepers, or pusher bars, not cultivators, plows, or harvesters. Seats were upholstered and padded, and options included a swingaway seat hinge as well as an offset mount to make it easier to do the maneuvering in reverse required of industrial work

1939 Model BWH Styled
One of the next projects on John Boehm's list is his 1939 Styled BWH, number 94741. As time permitted, development from Deere and from Dreyfuss progressed on the styled tractors. But the basics were here: the air-intake and exhaust pipes were aligned, and the hood was redesigned and tapered to improve visibility.

1938 Model B Special-Hi-Crop
Styled Model B Hi-Crops provided as much as 30in ground clearance from the factory. But for spraying tassled corn, something more was needed. An unknown Montana jobber reportedly built six of these, each with 6ft of ground clearance. Don Dufner of Buxton, North Dakota, owns this unique B, number 61338.

1940 Model BWH-40

Lester Layher's restored 1940 Model BWH-40, number 94435, was built very late in the nearly three-year production life of the model. The BWH was set to be replaced with Deere's new HWH, to be introduced specifically for the California markets in 1941. Still waiting to be introduced was a comfortable operator's seat.

Following pages

1944 Model BO Lindeman crawler

BO tractors were sold without tires to Jesse Lindeman in Yakima, Washington, to fit steel crawler tracks and gears. This crawler, number 333787, owned by Harold Schultz of Ollie, Iowa, was shipped on rubber pads to the US Navy to use for scraping clean the holds of its ships. Schultz's 1945 BR, number 334818, is at left.

1948 Model AO
The electrified AO used a Delco starter and generator, but spark was still generated by a magneto. The Wico Model X magneto and Schebler's DLTX carburetor were long-term carryovers on Deere's tractors. The AO stood only 44in tall to the top of the seat, compared with a regular A at 60in to the top of the seat.

*Y*ou've no idea of the great forward strides John Deere has made in general-purpose farm power until you see and drive one of these new "A," "B," or "G" Tractors for the first time

—A, B and G Series brochure

1948 Model AO
By 1948, Deere's Model AO and most other models were offered with optional or standard electric starter, generator, and lighting. Yet curiously, the orchard versions of the Model A tractors were among the last to be "styled" by Henry Dreyfuss Associates. Flat front radiators remained until the final series beginning in 1949.

Right
1948 Model AO
AO air intakes were mounted flush to the hood while the exhaust exited either alongside the engine or piped down below the rear axle and out the rear of the tractor. AO tractors remained in production until mid-1953. This 1948 example, number 209525, is owned by Frank Bettancourt.

1952 Model AH

The 5.50x6.75in engine running at 975rpm produced 26.7 drawbar horsepower and 33.8 horsepower on the belt pulley. A Delco electric system provided starter, generator, and distributor. Deere retained the Schebler DLTX carburetor. With its six-speed transmission and maze-like shift pattern, the AH topped out at 11mph.

Left
1952 Model AH

Styled Hi-Crop versions of the Model A were only produced in 1951 and 1952. These giants stood 96in to the top of the air intake and exhaust stacks. A full 30in was available under the rear differential, 35in under the front axle. AH models rode on 7.50x20in front tires and 12.4x38in rears.

1952 Model AH

Dreyfuss attended to the tractor front and to the operator's platform with a vastly improved seat and larger foot platform. His designers also reorganized the back end, changing the location and appearance of hydraulic fittings to ease and simplify their usage. Frank Bettancourt owns this example, number 682320.

59

Chapter 5

Expanding the Lines

Models L, LA, G, H and M

The introduction of mechanization was a mixed blessing to American farmers. At the turn of the century only the largest operators owned or hired steam traction engines for sod busting, planting, and harvesting. The other millions of family farms operated with horses, mules, or oxen for crop work. The fuel for these animals was allocated from the total farm acreage, about one-fifth of the land. Early gasoline tractors could do more work and do it faster. But the horses were already paid for and ate from farm produce; the tractors had to be purchased in town and fed by fuel from town.

World War I changed the equations dramatically. Not only were a million and more men required but hundreds of thousands of horses were needed to haul artillery and other loads. While many of the men came home, many of the horses did not.

When the war ended, the economy reeled like a drunk trying to regain its sober footing. More than 100 manufacturers failed: from more than 180 in business in 1920, only thirty-seven remained in 1930. The economy had already toppled in October 1929, and it quickly took another dozen makers with it. Those who survived did so by responding to the needs of a market with fewer able-bodied men to work and a growing population to feed. While the number of large farms increased, the United States was still a nation of small farms that produced the food. Manufacturers—Deere and International Harvester most effectively—responded with smaller machines for these farms. Advertisements suggested that the farm

1938 Model L Unstyled
The first Model L tractors were unstyled, introduced in 1938. They used a Hercules upright-mounted 3.0x4.0 two-cylinder engine, and fewer than 1,500 were produced. Intended to pull one 12in plow, the Hercules engine rated 9.1 drawbar and 10.4 belt horsepower. This example, number 621098, is owned by Walter and Bruce Keller.

1946 Model L Styled
Tony Dieter is a blur of motion, cranking over Bob Pollock's 1946 Styled Model L, number 641970. Deere equipped the Ls with electric start but knew that batteries go flat. A single-plow tractor, the Model L used Deere's 3.25x4.00in twin cylinder, producing 7 horsepower at the drawbar and 10.4 horsepower on the belt at 1480rpm.

draft animals could be sold to pay for the tractors. Farmers were told that the added acreage now returned to production for profit rather than for feed would more than compensate for fuel and maintenance costs. As the economy began its recovery, the census of farm tractors reached more than 2.4 million, while the population of horses dropped nearly one-fourth, to barely 12 million. It took five horses to pull the same two-bottom plow that Deere's Model A or GP could do. But it was usually only when the

horses died of disease, old age, or unforeseen circumstances such as lightning strikes that farmers relented and went to machines.

The Model B tractor had been intended for those smallest farms that still relied on two-horse teams, which constituted a substantial proportion of American farmland. Model Bs were even referred to as Deere's garden tractor for a short while. But Deere felt there was a need for something even smaller: a one-plow tractor for the last holdouts. Development mod-

1941 Model LA

In 1941, Deere replaced the Styled Model L with the Model LA. Henry Dreyfuss Associates did the design work, creating an easily recognizable shape with the little tractor. With new sheet metal came Deere's own engine, a 3.50x4.00in upright twin. This example was the first built, number 1001, belonging to Walter and Bruce Keller.

1941 Model HWH
John Boehm's 1941 HWH, number 36455, waits for sunrise. Deere's Model H was intended for the last farmers holding onto horsepower. With Deere's 3.60x5.00in two-cylinder producing 12.5 drawbar and just 14.8 belt pulley horsepower, this was the company's smallest row-crop tractor. Fitted with only a three-speed transmission, a road speed of 8.5mph was still possible using the governor override and running the engine at 1800rpm.

els were referred to as the Model Y; its production name was the Model L.

Most of the company development money in 1936 was going to Theo Brown to perfect the Model A and B. So Willard Nordenson, a former Deere & Company engineer, was rehired and given the challenge to produce a tractor out of existing parts and pieces for large estates, golf courses, and even cemeteries. Nordenson went outside Deere for a Hercules two-cylinder engine that he mounted upright. He coupled it to Ford's Model A automobile transmission. The familiar H-shift pattern and foot clutch

were selling points to nonagriculture operators who had previous experience with automobiles but none with tractors. To keep the Model L compact in length, the engine and operator were offset on opposite sides of the centerline.

Henry Dreyfuss got to the Model L nearly from the beginning, and while the tractor was introduced Unstyled in 1938, it was replaced in 1939 with the Styled version. Unlike the A and B, the Unstyled L was discontinued. When the Model LA was introduced in 1941 to replace the Model L, the Hercules engine was supplanted by Deere's own two-cylinder, producing nearly 50 percent more power. Deere—and many farmers—knew it cost more than the $545 price of an LA to replace a team of horses.

This was a period of expansion for Deere's tractor line. While Henry Dreyfuss remodeled and rehabilitated the Model A and B tractors, the company was testing and proving its little Model L; it also introduced two new general purpose tractors, the Model G and H. The G was conceived as a three-plow powerhouse. Curiously, the G did not replace the three-plow-rated Model D, and the G had not been worked over by Dreyfuss and Associates prior to its introduction. The H, conceived as a one-plow tractor, was advertised as the right machine to choose for a second tractor. Eventually, the Model G and H tractors—as well as the Styled and Unstyled A and B models—were offered in standard-tread or row-crop configurations, as Narrows with a single front tire, with extended front axles as Wide versions, and as high-clearance models called Hi-Crops. Deere offered a tractor for every crop, every function, and every farm.

1941 Model HWH

The HWH was nicknamed the California High Crop; about 125 were produced only in 1941. Model H tractors differed from other models by using rear brakes on the axles rather than onto bullgears functioning as brake drums. The belt pulley drove off the camshaft. HWHs rode on 8-38 rear tires and provided nearly 24in clearance. The HWH stood 55in tall to the top of the hood, 119in long, and 79in wide. It weighed 2,389 pounds.

1947 Model MI
In 1947 Deere introduced its Model M, to replace the
Model LA and the H. Using its 4.00x4.00in engine
mounted vertically, the M was then offered in industrial,
tricycle, crawler, and regular configurations. This 1947
Industrial, number 10822, owned by Bob Pollock of
Denison, Iowa, was one of slightly more than 1,000
produced.

The Second World War interrupted Deere's
plans to introduce new tractors and increase
prices. Washington rationed rubber and steel,
which further curtailed Moline's plans. Yet the
company knew that development must continue so new products would be ready when the

Right
1952 Model MC
Model M Crawlers were produced from 1949 through
1952. The prototypes, tested for three years before
production, were developed by BO crawler inventor Jesse
Lindeman. Deere purchased Lindeman's company in
1946, moving its operations to Dubuque, Iowa, where
the MC was assembled. This model, number 16386,
belongs to Bob Pollock.

war ended. A new plant in Dubuque, Iowa, was ready and production began at the war's end on the replacement for the Model H and L.

The 1947 Model M introduced Touch-O-Matic hydraulics and the Quick-Tatch mounting system, and it reintroduced to John Deere tractors the vertically mounted engine seen previously only on the Model L and on the first Deere All-Wheel Drive thirty years before. Labeled a one/two plow tractor, it was aimed at farmers hit hardest by the war, those who lost manpower or horsepower. The M enabled small farm owners to get by without a hired hand. A new line of implements was offered, scaled to fit the Model M. The Quick-Tatch mounting system and Touch-O-Matic hydraulics greatly increased the tractor/implement flexibility and ease of operation.

The operator's comfort was paramount with the M. The seat, already improved on Dreyfuss-styled tractors over the early steel seats on early Model Ds, was now made adjustable, air cushioned, and fitted with a padded seat back. Dreyfuss' designers invented a telescoping steering wheel shaft to move the wheel a foot further back when the operator stood. The M tractor was offered as a row-crop version with a widely adjustable rear track width and as a crawler, the MC. The MC replaced Lindeman's BO crawlers and was initially engineered by the Washington inventor. Just before the introduction of the MC, Deere acquired Lindeman's company and moved it all to Dubuque.

1953 Model G Hi-Crop
The Model G was introduced in 1937 but Styled Hi-Crops did not appear before 1951. A strong three-plow tractor, the 6.125x7.00in engine produced 34.5 drawbar horsepower and 38.1 pulley horsepower at 975rpm. Maurice Horn's 1953 model, number 63674, came standard with electric starter and headlights.

Chapter 6

More Power

Model R, Number Series, 20 Series and 30 Series

Following World War II, engines took on greater importance. Before the war, Deere's two-cylinder engines seemed perfectly adequate. They always behaved reliably. But farmers and hired hands who went to war drove four- and six-cylinder trucks and Jeeps, and when they returned home, two-cylinders seemed somehow a little shy.

The sound of Deere's two-cylinder engines was familiar and comfortable to many farmsteads. It had even become a form of communication. Wives heard their husbands stop to chat over the fence with the implement salesperson or with another farmer; the noise under load was much deeper, more metallic. And when they heard the engine popping quickly at midday, it signaled time to put lunch on the table.

But Deere had nearly reached the limits of reliable power from its two-cylinder engines. When 35 horsepower pulled two plows through the soil, a 6.00in bore and stroke was fine. When 35 horsepower was needed just to run the hydraulics, engineers found a limit to how far they could make a spark fly across a huge piston. There was also a limit to how long and wide a tractor would fit between some crop rows.

Diesels were introduced at the turn of the century and perfected for tractor use in the early 1930s. They were adapted to Deere prototypes. Tested for thousands of hours, the engines were introduced to farmers in 1949 as the new Model R tractors. Aggressively styled to reflect their substantial power, the Model Rs also introduced live power takeoff (PTO), which ran independent of ground speed, and a new hydraulic sys-

1956 Model 420 Hi-Crop
Introduced in 1955, the Model 420 replaced the Model 40 Series tractors. Cylinder bore was increased from 4.00in to 4.25in, increasing horsepower by nearly 20 percent. Live power takeoff was standard on most versions, and three-point draft control was optional in the dual Touch-O-Matic system.

1948 Model D Styled
Henry Dreyfuss styled the Model D tractors to emphasize the strength and power of the original while improving its functions. Harv Monesmith's 1948 model, number 178263, shows Dreyfuss' success. The 130in long, 5,269 pound tractor looks like it could burst its skin. Massive Goodyear 13.5x28s add to the impression.

tem called Powr-Trol, which adjusted the implement as the tractor pitched and rolled.

In the early 1950s, Deere & Company finally retired the letter-series tractors. More than 600,000 Model As and Bs had sold. The letters were replaced by five numbered models from 40 through 80. Horsepower ranged from 17 through 46. Both horizontal and upright engines were used, with new carburetion or fuel injection for the diesels. Fuel options included Liquid Propane Gas (LPG) as well as gasoline, distillates, and diesel. Even power steering was optional.

In 1956, the entire line was replaced again. Power increased and the tractors' designations changed. The series now ranged from Model 320 up through 820, and power increased nearly 20 percent across the line. The entire group

looked like it matched; Dreyfuss' designers had been in from the start. And again in 1958 when the entire lineup jumped again (330 through 830), the predominant changes were visual appearance and operator comfort.

No mechanical changes were offered in these new "30 Series" tractors. This was because drastic mechanical changes were being perfected. Deere was looking far into the future.

1954 Model 70 Hi-Crop
With 32in ground clearance under the rear differential, the Model 70 Hi-Crop gave the operator high visibility. Using the 6.125x7.00in engine at 975rpm as with the Model G, the 70 rated 31.1 drawbar and 38.4 belt horsepower. This 1954 Model 70, number 7009419, was the third all-fuel Hi-Crop produced, and belongs to Tony Dieter of Vail, Iowa

73

*The new John Deere Model 80
Diesel brings you big capacity
at rock-bottom operating costs
—Model 80 Diesel brochure*

1955 Model 70 Diesel Cotton Picker Model 22
Fitted to Model 60 or 70 tractors, Deere's Model 22 Air-Trol cotton pickers operated with the tractor running in reverse at 3.5 or 4mph respectively. A remote operator's platform sat up behind the normal position. Larry Maasdam of Clarion, Iowa, owns this and a Model 22 picker on a Diesel 60.

Right
1955 Model 70 Diesel Cotton Picker Model 22
Mounted on a narrow front Model 70, the Air-Trol was capable of loading 1,200 pounds of picked cotton. Onboard hydraulics lifted and dumped the load. Below, the bare tractor weighed another 7,135 pounds, not including the weight of the Air-Trol. Deere engineering met the challenge of the apparatus without breaking tractor frames.

1956 Model 420 Hi-Crop
The Hi-Crop models were introduced in 1956 and offered 32in ground clearance beneath the axles. They were heavily promoted for tomato growers in the west by

Deere dealers. Track width was 48in. This example, number 105154, purchased new by Frank Bettancourt, still carries the 52-0 bar for tomato cultivation.

Left
1956 Model 420 Hi-Crop
With bean rows on the horizon in central California, a three-row cultivator hangs from the 420 Hi-Crop. It calls to mind Deere & Company's earliest row-crop Model C. Engineer Theo Brown was criticized for inventing the three-row cultivator in 1928. Fifty-five years later, on a thirty-seven-year old tractor, the rig seems fine.

M odern methods spell the difference between profit and loss in today's farming operations —Models 520, 620 & 720 brochure

1957 Model 620 Hi-Crop
The Model 620 Hi-Crops were offered with gasoline,
tractor fuel, or LPG-burning engines from their
introduction in 1951. Meant for tall crops such as sugar
cane, cotton, or even flowers, the Hi-Crops were not tall
enough for corn. Bob Pollock's 1957 model, number
6215383, was one of the seventeen tractor-fuel Hi-Crops.

Left
1960 Model 830
Everything about the Model 830 is impressive, its size and
scale in particular. It's only a slight photographic illusion
that the tractor seems larger than the house behind it. The
830 was nearly 143in long, 80in wide, and 81in tall. Its
rear tires were 23:1x26 rice specials. Its six-speed
transmission allowed a transport speed of 12.25mph.

1959 Model 530 Standard

The Model 530 was only an interim model, to placate buyers while Deere forged ahead with plans. It was only offered in 1959 (this example, number 5302325, is owned by Maurice Horn) and hinted at Dreyfuss styling to come: sloping auto-style dashboard, quad headlights in the modern rear fenders, better seat, and much more.

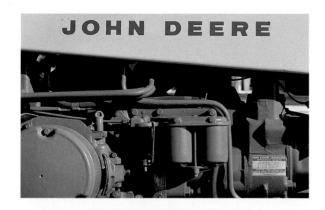

1960 Model 830

Deere's giant, the Model 830, was the natural successor to the early Model D. By 1958, Deere's powerhouse was 6.125x8.00in bore and stroke and ran on diesel fuel. It produced 69.7 horsepower at the drawbar and 75.6 horsepower on the PTO shaft. The rice version, as shown here with the hydraulic Powr-Trol system, weighed just about 9,290 pounds. It sold for nearly $6,850.

1960 Model 830

Frank Bettancourt's giant 1960 Model 830, number 8306051, was a rice version, equipped with special equipment to protect brakes and electrical systems from the rice paddy water. It is attached to a John Deere Number 8 "Three by Four" 16in plow. Three by four refers to three main plow beams plus an extension.

Chapter 7

New Generations

Four-Cylinder and Six-Cylinder Tractors

Deere's engineering department and Drey-fuss and Associates were invited in during mid-1953 to discuss the company's "New Generation of Power." Following decades of statements and defenses, protests and promises that Deere would never abandon the two-cylinder engine, plans were underway to replace everything with four- and six-cylinder diesels. But not only the engines were to be replaced. The engineers and designers were told to start with a clean sheet of paper.

Everything Deere had done since 1923 was only a modification or an improvement on what Witry and Leavitt had originated. Now the engineers were told they were to reinvent the farm tractor. Knowing what they knew, they were to use their imagination to guess what they would need in the future.

This project was one of the best kept secrets in American industrial history. And when Deere let it out of the bag on Monday, August 29, 1960, Deere-Day in Dallas had just about as

much impact as D-Day in Normandy. And the result was similarly dramatic.

By August 1960, Deere & Company had manufactured more than 1,450,000 two-cylinder tractors. The tractor division had surpassed expectations, going from the board of directors' single greatest fear to become the corporation's single largest profit maker. Deere's two-cylinder tractors had appealed to farmers for decades because of their simplicity and ease of repair.

The New Generation of Power tractors ranged from a 35 horsepower four-cylinder diesel (or gasoline) Model 1010 up to an 80

1960 Model 4020 Pedal Toy
Deere & Company anticipated a hard sell when it discontinued its long-lived two-cylinder engines for its new four- and six-cylinder models in the New Generation of Power. But it made use of several innovative marketing tools, a comic series in its magazine, *The Furrow*, and pedal toys to appeal to the youngsters who were their future customers.

1960 Model 4020 Pedal Toy
Deere had produced toy pedal-powered tractors of its current production since the early 1950s. The toys were a way for youngsters to have a John Deere just like Dad or Grandpa. With the arrival of the New Generation of Power tractors, the company commemorated the new models with Model 4020 Diesel Standards.

horsepower six-cylinder diesel Model 4010. Within two years, a 100 horsepower seven-plow-rated six-cylinder Model 5010 increased the company range. A year later, designations changed slightly and power increased again; by 1965, Deere's most powerful tractor, the 5020, boasted 133 horsepower.

As family farms consolidated—or sold out to corporate giants—and as yields from hybrid seeds improved and acreage increased, the quest for more power was relentless. In 1969, Deere's giant 5020 produced 141 horsepower and its 4020 and 3020 tractors were offered with optional hydraulic-powered front-wheel-drive assist. This was not quite a full-fledged four-wheel drive, but it went a long way to getting the power more effectively to the ground. Tur-bochargers, not yet a trendy performance fea-

1965 Model 3020 Grove and Orchard
Orchard tractors always represented "Styling" at its most stylish. The New Generation tractors continued the rule. Introduced in 1963, the 20 Series of four-cylinder diesels with 4.25x4.75in engines produced 57.1 drawbar and 65.3 PTO horsepower. This sleek example, number 81139, is owned by Barry Stelford of Urbana, Illinois.

ture on passenger cars, appeared on Deere's diesels and eventually produced 135 horsepower from the Model 4520.

Dreyfuss' designers had produced a distinctive-looking tractor with a curved hood. This provided an optical trick-of-the-eye where, no matter what combination of front and rear wheel sizes were used, the tractor always looked nearly level. Many features, designed to improve operator safety and tractor performance were equally subtle. But another of Dreyfuss' innovations was much more apparent—and much less popular.

Farmers understood the logic behind roll-over bars on tractors. But they all believed it would be the other guy who would need it. So when Deere's tractors were available only with the roll bar, farmers went looking elsewhere.

Not until Deere offered its research, design, and technology to its competition in exchange for an agreement to install roll bars universally did farmers began to accept the inevitability of safety, and sales returned to Deere.

Safety went the next big step in Deere's Generation II tractors: they included air conditioning and heating. Inside a glass-enclosed "SoundGard" cab equipped with a radio/cassette deck, operator safety became downright appealing. Increased power went with it. Deere's largest articulated four-wheel-drive tractors, fitted with Synchro-Range transmissions (sixteen speeds) with the Perma-Clutch—a hydraulic wet-plate clutch, essentially making it behave like an automatic transmission—225 horsepower was comfortably available from the Model 8630.

In the 1980s the quest for more power resulted in two more cylinders. Weighing in at 37,700lb, wearing eight tires, and boasting a 955ci V-8 diesel engine with intercooled turbocharger, the Model 8850 produced 304 horsepower. And then in 1992, it started all over again.

The new 6000 and 7000 series tractors ranged from 66 horsepower to 145 horsepower from their turbocharged diesels. These New

1975 Model 2630 and Model 348 Bailer
Lewis Denlinger watches while his Deere Model 348 bailer launches another one into the hay wagon behind him. Denlinger operates his Dubuque-built 1975 Model 2630 near his home in Paradise, Pennsylvania. His 2630 is fitted with the Roll-Gard roll-over bar and roof. The 2630 produced 58.2 drawbar horsepower at 2500rpm.

Breed of Power tractors feature the most sophisticated and advanced engines, drivetrains, hydraulic management systems, and cabs available in the agricultural implement marketplace. They were Deere's first tractors built on an independent chassis. An engine rebuild years from now would simply entail a quick drive to the local shop and an engine exchange. The new machines were designed and manufactured to be used worldwide and to meet any foreign regulation with very little modification. Operating controls featured international symbols to designate their various operations and functions.

Deere & Company is now in first place in tractor sales and has been since soon after the introduction of the New Generation tractors in 1960. The many enthusiasts who have established the hobby of collecting antique tractors were originally operators. People started collecting because one tractor or another was "the first one the family owned," "the model my grandfather used," or "the one I learned to farm with." John Deere collectors with foresight are gathering up and restoring New Generation of Power tractors. A freshly redone Model 3020 Orchard and Grove tractor is nearly as appealing as the Model 60 Orchard or a Model AOS Orchard Streamline. It is not too difficult to imagine that somewhere the young child of a John Deere collector has already cast a long hard look at Dad's New Breed Model 7800 and has wondered silently how it will look in the collection in about thirty years.

1977 Model 4440
Over rolling fields of South Dakota, a Deere Model 4440, introduced in 1977, works the soil with a Model 235 three-section 26ft-wide folding disk. The 4440, powered by Deere's six-cylinder turbocharged 4.57x4.75in diesel, produced 112.6 drawbar horsepower—all of it needed to pull disks capable of 100lb/disk pressure

1979 Model 4840 and Model 9600 Combine
Lester Layher's 1979 Model 4840 turbocharged and intercooled six-cylinder diesel waits to unload the auger cart behind. In the background, son Harland begins another round with their Model 9600 combine. The tractor produces 157.1 drawbar horsepower at 2200rpm. In tandem with the combine, they harvest 3,000 bushels of corn per hour.

*P*ictures and words are no
substitute for the "feel" and
thrill of actually operating an All-
New John Deere Tractor in the field
—Models 2010, 3010
and 4010 brochure

1983 Model 4650

Glen and Chuck Wilder operate a Model 4650 to harvest beets near Crookston, Minnesota. The 4650 was introduced in 1983 and used Deere's 466ci 4.57x4.75in six-cylinder turbocharged and intercooled diesel to produce 145.6 drawbar horsepower at 2200rpm. The 118in wheelbase tractor weighed 19,615 pounds.

1989 Model 4455
Marlan Dufault works a Model 4455 through sugar beets near Crookston, Minnesota. The 4455 was introduced in 1989 and had the same engine as the 4440; but with larger valves its power was increased to 128.8 horsepower at 2200rpm on the drawbar. Dufault uses a beet lifter behind the sixteen-speed Quad-Range transmission tractor.

1989 Model AMT 626

The AMT line, All Materials Transports, was introduced in 1987 beginning with the AMT 600. The AMT 626 was introduced in late 1989, meant for nurseries and small orchards and farms. Produced in Canada at the John Deere Welland Works, the five-wheeled machines use a Kawasaki motorcycle engine driven through a viscous clutch.

Right

1989 Model 8760 and Model 635 Disk harrow

John Deere's Model 635 disk harrow will stretch 31ft across the field when unfolded. Robert Paschen's 1989 Model 8760 has adequate power for the load: the 619ci turbocharged-intercooled diesel with 5.12x5.00in bore and stroke produced 240.2 drawbar horsepower at 2100rpm. Weighing 32,695 pounds, it was rated to pull 32,880 pounds!

1990 Model 4455 Castor/Action MFWD
Castor/Action Mechanical Front Wheel Drive not only
gave farmers increased traction in all soil conditions, but it
also greatly increased the maneuverability of longer-
wheelbase machines. Paul Eickert operates a 1990
Castor/Action MFWD Model 4455 with a Deere Model
2810 four-bottom plow to prepare for corn planting near
Brillion, Wisconsin.

Model 8760
Jim Henkel prepares to disk one of Robert Paschen's
fields near Logansport, Indiana. Running at 5.4mph at
2100rpm, forty acres takes about two hours. Deere's
Model 8760 used a twenty-four-speed PowrSync
transmission to perfectly match engine torque to ground
speed and drawbar load. Tires are dual 18.4x42 all
around.

Index